INFORMATION LITERACY IN THE DIGITAL AGE

by Laura Perdew

CONTENT CONSULTANT

Leslie F. Stebbins
Director for Research
Consulting Services for Education (CS4Ed)

Essential Library

An Imprint of Abdo Publishing | abdopublishing.com

abdopublishing.com

Published by Abdo Publishing, a division of ABDO, PO Box 398166, Minneapolis, Minnesota 55439. Copyright © 2017 by Abdo Consulting Group, Inc. International copyrights reserved in all countries. No part of this book may be reproduced in any form without written permission from the publisher. Essential Library™ is a trademark and logo of Abdo Publishing.

Printed in the United States of America, North Mankato, Minnesota
052016
092016

THIS BOOK CONTAINS
RECYCLED MATERIALS

Cover Photo: Shutterstock Images
Interior Photos: iStockphoto, 5, 7, 13, 18, 23, 25, 33, 35, 41, 47, 86; Susan Chiang/iStockphoto, 10, 31; Corbis, 15; Keystone View Company/Library of Congress, 16; Arda Guldogan/iStockphoto, 28; Public Domain, 37; Tobias Hase/Picture-Alliance/DPA/AP Images, 43; Ugurhan Betin/iStockphoto, 44; Ricky Carioti/The Washington Post/Getty Images, 49; The George F. Landegger Collection of Connecticut Photographs in the Carol M. Highsmith's America, Library of Congress, 51; iPhone/Alamy, 55; Walter McBride/Corbis, 57; Narciso Contreras/AP Images, 59; Universal Images Group/Getty Images, 61; Ng Han Guan/AP Images, 63; Chris Pizzello/Invision/AP, 65; Paul Sakuma/AP Images, 68, 75; Boisiere/SIPA/AP Images, 71; Aidan Monaghan/TM/20th Century Fox Film Corps/Everett Collection, 73; Tom Gralish/MCT/Newscom, 78; Marcelo Hernandez/AP Images, 81; Bob Herbert/The Wilmington News-Journal/AP Images, 83; John Bazemore/AP Images, 85; Chris Schmidt/iStockphoto, 91; Blend Images/Alamy, 93; Shannon Trust/PA Wire URN:5811731/AP Images, 95; Rob Swanson/AP Images, 97

Editor: Elizabeth Dingmann Schneider
Series Designer: Craig Hinton

Publisher's Cataloging in Publication Data

Names: Perdew, Laura, author.
Title: Information literacy in the digital age / by Laura Perdew.
Description: Minneapolis, MN : Abdo Publishing, [2017] | Series: Essential library of the information age | Includes bibliographical references and index.
Identifiers: LCCN 2015960313 | ISBN 9781680782851 (lib. bdg.) | ISBN 9781680774740 (ebook)
Subjects: LCSH: Digital media--Juvenile literature. | Information literacy--Juvenile literature. | Media literacy--Juvenile literature. | Internet--Juvenile literature.
Classification: DDC 302--dc23
LC record available at http://lccn.loc.gov/2015960313

CONTENTS

CHAPTER 1

LITERACY IN THE INFORMATION AGE

Imagine the discovery of a new primary color. As an addition to the known primary colors of red, blue, and yellow, this fourth color would change much of what is known about color theory. In 2006, a Wikipedia editor found an article about this very subject on the Internet. The article claimed that 1960s counterculture icon Timothy Leary had discovered a color called gendale. The editor promptly added the information to Leary's Wikipedia biography. Not too long afterward, the *Guardian*, a prominent British newspaper read by people around the world, reported the discovery as well. The article was read and reread countless times, and the news passed from person to person. And with that, the concept of four primary colors became fact.

The only problem was, it wasn't true. It was part of a social experiment by Kyle Stoneman, creator of the website Gullible.info. Amazingly, fact-checkers at the *Guardian* failed to catch the mistake. Stoneman himself even said this information was untrue, pointing out that he had been the one to make it up. Yet for three

Articles on Wikipedia are written and edited by volunteers from around the world.

WIKIPEDIA

English
e Free Encyclopedia
3 560 000+ articles

日本語
フリー百科事典
734 000+ 記事

sch
zyklopädie
0+ Artikel

Esp
La enciclo

als
die libre

articles

aliano
lopedia libera

4 000+ voci

Py

Nederlands
De vrije encyclo
672 000+ artikel

Pr
A ent

Polski
Wolna encyklopedia
775 000+ haseł

...ch · suchen · rechercher · szukaj · ricerca · 検索 · buscar · busca · ...
...ca · suk · пошук · haku · hledání · keresés · tìm kiếm · căutare · 찾기 · ...
...ğu · претрага · paieška · hľadať · suk · שיפוש · بحث · Пошук · ...

English

GULLIBLE.INFO

The first post on Gullible.info by then 19-year-old university student Kyle Stoneman read: "Everything on Gullible.info is true."[2] Stoneman, concerned with people's willingness to believe everything they read, started Gullible.info on September 19, 2004, as a social experiment. The site quickly gained popularity as he provided the public with new and amazing "facts," including trivia on an array of subjects from cats to presidents to the life expectancy of a sneaker. And, despite the name of the website itself, people believed what they read. His experiment highlights the critical need for information literacy in an age when information can be created and shared by just about anyone.

months the *Guardian* failed to retract what it had written.

In a world where information is increasingly easy to create and access, information literacy is more critical than ever before. The *Guardian* should have uncovered Stoneman's joke long before the mainstream public was gossiping about the discovery of a new primary color.

WHAT IS INFORMATION LITERACY?

In the information age, the amount of available information continues to grow exponentially. Experts believe that by 2020, new information will be created at a rate 44 times greater than in 2009.[1] As such, information literacy is much more complex than it was even 50 years ago. Being literate used to mean being able to read and write. Information literacy involved the simple act of finding appropriate reference material. Now the resources themselves have changed, and so have the filtering

Advancing technology creates access to an ever-increasing amount of new information.

processes that determine what information a learner can access. Where learners of the past relied more heavily on publishers and librarians to filter the information available to them, today's learner must be able to locate correct information amidst an endless tangle of possibilities. More important, learners must also possess the critical thinking skills necessary to choose, assess, and use information successfully.

❝ To prosper in the digital age, people must become masters of information. ❞ [3]

—The National Forum on Information Literacy

Information literacy in the digital age is an integrated

set of skills. It includes recognizing a need for information and creating appropriate research questions, locating relevant sources and information, critically evaluating the information, and communicating and sharing findings effectively and responsibly. With the explosive growth and increasing complexity of the information landscape, understanding how to navigate and critically analyze information is the foundation for future success. The key is that today's learners must know how to learn.

BECOMING INFORMATION LITERATE

Information literacy begins with an awareness of the need for information. Many times teachers generate this need by assigning research papers or projects. The need can also stem from personal interests and the desire to know more about a subject. It could even be as simple as wanting to know the day's weather forecast!

Once there is a need, individuals must be able to focus on exactly what must be learned. They should start by identifying essential questions that will guide their research process. Once the decision has been made to buy a car, for example, the buyer must define the need for information based on her budget and interests. For instance, there is no need to research expensive foreign cars if funds are limited or to look at an old truck if gas mileage is a consideration. The car buyer must then identify what she does need to know and find potential sources for that information.

The next step is to identify and access correct information. This involves sifting through many print, digital, and other types of sources. Perhaps an Internet search would be most appropriate, or perhaps an interview or field study is needed. Maybe books or journals are best suited to the project in question. The car buyer might read reports from consumer organizations or even talk to a mechanic familiar with certain cars. She would also probably search online for detailed information or even reviews from other car owners.

While information is collected, it must also be evaluated. This is especially true in an age of dramatic increase in the quantity of available information. Experts aren't the only people who create and share information. Anyone can generate and distribute content using social media and messaging platforms. Just as in the case with the *Guardian* and the new color gendale, information seekers must figure out if the information is believable, timely, and relevant. In order to avoid bias, it is also important to take into account the point of view from which the information is shared.

Before visiting car dealerships, a shopper may conduct an online search to learn about important factors such as gas mileage or safety ratings.

Finally, armed with correct, reliable information, individuals must decide how to use what they have found, and they must do so in an ethical way. This could include collaborating with others, solving problems, developing new ideas, formulating opinions, summarizing and communicating findings, or creating products. No matter the method of sharing new information, communication in the digital age requires the practice of ethical behaviors, such as following copyright laws and respecting the personal rights of members of an online community.

People who are information literate have learned how to learn. They know how to wade through vast quantities of information in order to find correct information and determine its legitimacy. Information literacy can keep people from believing untrue things—such as the discovery of a new primary color.

INFOBESITY

Infobesity is a condition that occurs when people consume such large amounts of information that it has a negative effect on their well-being and ability to concentrate. The term is a blend of *information* and *obesity*, drawing a parallel between overconsumption of information and overconsumption of food. The Internet offers constant access to information, and many people are obsessed with consuming as much as they can. Just as eaters must make healthful choices about the food they eat, so too must Internet users make good choices about the information they consume. Giving into the craving can leave users listless, indecisive, and ultimately uninformed.

NATIONAL INFORMATION LITERACY AWARENESS MONTH

President Barack Obama was the first US president to utilize the power of social media in the digital age. Obama also understood the dire need for individuals to be able to manage and evaluate the onslaught of information available 24 hours a day. On October 1, 2009, Obama declared October to be National Information Literacy Awareness Month. This proclamation, Obama said, "highlights the need for all Americans to be adept in the skills necessary to effectively navigate the Information Age."[4] He emphasized that all Americans must adjust to this new reality so they can separate truth from fiction. This ability is both an important job skill and a key aspect of participation in a democratic society. National Information Literacy Awareness Month underscores the vital importance of information literacy. Likewise, Obama's proclamation was a call to educators to teach students the information literacy skills necessary for a successful future.

Obama has embraced social media platforms, including Twitter, as a way to communicate with the public.

 Search   Home   F

Barack Obama

@BarackObama Washington, DC

44th President of the United States
http://www.barackobama.com

 Follow

Tweets   Favorites   Following   Followers   Lists

 BarackObama Barack Obama
Thanking police officers for their service. Watch live at www.wh.gov/live.
2 hours ago

 BarackObama Barack Obama
It's time to fix our immigration system - and Washingto
unless you lead. Add your name to a call for reform:
http://OFA.BO/QTJwi4
11 May

 BarackObama Barack Obama
"So we're going to keep fighting for the Dream Act.
keep up the fight for reform." #immigration
10 May

 BarackObama Barack Obama
"I don't believe the United States of America shou
...ting families. That's not right. T

CHAPTER 2

THE HISTORY OF LITERACY

Even when the United States was still in its infancy, the framers of the nation's constitution recognized the power of literacy to create a strong democracy. Freedom of individual expression and freedom of the press became part of the First Amendment to the US Constitution. Yet Thomas Jefferson also recognized that in order to make freedom of the press meaningful, the United States needed a literate population to read what was printed. In 1816, he wrote to a fellow legislator that in a nation "where the press is free, and every man able to read, all is safe."[1] Jefferson was also among the first to propose a public school system in the United States to teach basic reading, writing, and arithmetic.

The greatest obstacle to Jefferson's vision of public schools was that up until the 1900s, the United States was extremely rural. Its populations were distributed over vast regions. Centralized schools were often difficult to establish, especially in the rugged West. Before the 1900s, most children were taught in the home. Sometimes teachers traveled from home to home, but more often children learned reading and writing from other family members.

Thomas Jefferson believed literacy was necessary for a nation to have a well-informed public.

In 1927, first-grade students worked on a project at a community school in Meadville, Pennsylvania.

As developing technology increased train travel and brought new factories to cities, more people moved to urban areas. As a result, community schools became more central to children's education. By 1916 there were as many as 200,000 schools across the country.[2]

Slowly more people migrated from rural areas, and by 1920 the majority of Americans lived in

"A look at the past can reveal how we can improve present and future literacy efforts."[3]

—Edward E. Gordon and Elaine H. Gordon, National Association of Secondary School Principals, November 2003

In 1900, a literate person was able to write his or her own name, which was
enough to enable individuals to function adequately in society. According
to these standards, almost 90 percent of the US population was literate.[4]
For decades, literacy statistics focused on level of education and on very
basic levels of reading and writing. By 1947, being literate in America meant
completing five or more years of school, and by 1993 it meant finishing
high school. Then, in 1993, the National Center for Education Statistics
adjusted its definition of literacy to include a wider range of skills needed
to accomplish literacy tasks at home, at school, and in the community.
According to the 2003 National Assessment of Adult Literacy (NAAL),
there is cause for concern about the literacy rates in the United States.
Fewer than 66 percent of the adult population can perform "moderately
challenging" or "complex and challenging" literacy activities.[5]

cities. Prior to this, all states had passed mandatory education laws.
This led to the evolution of high schools, which would teach math,
liberal arts, and science. These laws set out to ensure that everyone
in the United States has the right to a free, public education
supported by taxes.

INFORMATION EXPLOSION

Literacy rates in the United States have improved, but a new
problem has emerged. Individuals may be able to read and write,
but there is growing concern that many are not fluent enough
to navigate through the increasingly complex world of the
information age.

This shift is occurring as digital technology becomes
increasingly common and the amount of available information
grows. In the past, the focus of schools was to teach students to

Today's students must learn how to find and manage the ever-increasing amount of information available via digital technology.

read and write. In high schools, the main goal was to pass along advanced knowledge and facts that would help students succeed in future careers. Today's students still need to know how to read and write, but there is less of a need to memorize facts. Instead, students must know how to find and manage the explosion of information available to them.

The term *information explosion* was first used in 1941 as a means to explain the rapid increase in the amount of available data and information. And that was before the Internet, which was first put to use by government organizations in the 1980s. Since then people have used the Internet as a platform to discover, generate, and share ever-increasing amounts of information. In 2013, statistics revealed that 90 percent of the information in the world had been created within the previous two years.[6] That means since the beginning of humankind, up until 2011, humans created only 10 percent of the information available by 2013.[7] Experts predict the generation of information will continue to gain speed in years ahead.

CURRENT CONTEXT

In 1989, the US Presidential Committee on Information Literacy understood the changing dynamics of education in the new

NATIONAL LITERACY ACT OF 1991

As a whole, Americans are more literate and better educated than ever before. However, reports published in the second half of the 1900s revealed that a significant number of US adults did not have the literacy skills needed to function and participate in a modern world. This intensified the debate over how to address literacy in the information age. Literacy in the United States is a national concern that has both social and economic implications. As a result, Congress passed the National Literacy Act of 1991. The goal of the act is:

to enhance the literacy and basic skills of adults, to ensure that all adults in the United States acquire the basic skills necessary to function effectively and achieve the greatest possible opportunity in their work and in their lives, and to strengthen and coordinate adult literacy programs.[14]

The legislation increased funding for literacy programs and resources. The act also went beyond traditional literacy outreach. It included programs to promote literacy in the workplace as well as other adult education programs.

Information Age. In a report released in January of that year, the committee stated: "How our country deals with the realities of the Information Age will have enormous impact on our democratic way of life and on our nation's ability to compete internationally."[13] The committee's statement builds on the understanding of the US forefathers that a powerful, successful democracy depends on the literacy of its citizens.

Unfortunately, there is a digital divide in the United States and around the world, separating those with access to digital technology and the Internet from those without. In the United States, a 2015 report indicated certain sections of the population were more likely to have limited access to the Internet. The groups of people who were affected included African-American and Hispanic populations, as well as those living in rural areas. In addition, the report showed older, less wealthy, and less educated Americans also experienced more limited Internet access. In addition, ownership of devices such as smartphones, cell phones, tablets, and computers also varies by age, income, and level of education. The largest disparities were found among citizens aged 65 years and older, those earning less than $30,000 per year, and those without any college education.[15] These groups were less likely to own devices than other groups included in the study.[16]

Access to the Internet is one step toward an information literate population in the digital age. Another key is acknowledging the critical role of schools and universities in teaching information literacy skills. Moving literacy into the new millennium requires redefining what it means to do research. In the past, students did research by visiting the library, using encyclopedias, and reading textbooks. In the digital age, however, fewer and fewer students turn to books. Instead a search for information begins on the Internet, with search engines being the go-to resource.

Among today's students, to research often means to use the Google search engine. A 2012 Pew Research Center study revealed that when assigned a research task, teachers reported 94 percent of their students were "very likely" to use Google.[17] The second source students were most likely to use was Wikipedia, at 75 percent.[18] Unlike previous generations, students of the 2010s turned to printed books, textbooks, or librarians less than 20 percent of the time.[19] This indicates that students are using fewer

THE HISTORY OF SEARCH ENGINES

Long before Google and Yahoo were household names, Archie ruled the Internet. Created in 1990 by college student Alan Emtage, Archie was the world's first search engine. Yet Emtage didn't set out to create a multibillion-dollar industry or to revolutionize the way people sought information. He simply wanted to create a system to help students and faculty at McGill University in Montreal, Quebec, find software stored in standard network directory archives. The name "Archie" was derived from *archive*. At that time the Internet was still in its infancy, and making money from it was unheard of, so Emtage didn't patent his system.

edited, scholarly sources for information and instead are relying on the information that appears in a Google search.

Use of the Internet for research is much less time-consuming than in the past. Information on just about anything is available at any time. The key, however, is not just being able to find information, but knowing which types of information are reliable and where that information can be found.

Google is a common starting place for people who want to find a piece of information.

CHAPTER 3

THE NEW FACE
OF INFORMATION

nformation in the new millennium has a whole new look. The word *information* still means knowledge, facts, or details obtained about someone or something. But information has been restyled and given a new identity, making it an unrecognizable cousin of information before the advent of the Internet. And there is more of it in the world than ever before.

NO MORE SHELVES

It used to be that any information worth seeking could be found in a logical place such as a shelf or file system. Its location was determined by the specific category to which it belonged. Part of this system of categorizing and organizing information had to do with physical constraints. A book in a library has to go someplace, and it can only be in one place at a time.

Digital information is different. It challenges long-standing assumptions about how information should be organized, because in the digital world there are no physical constraints. Information can be in countless places and countless categories all at the same time. Shelves are no longer needed, and they have been replaced

In a physical library, information is carefully organized on shelves. Digital information is not limited by this physical constraint.

by links. Information seekers simply need to type in keywords for search engines to display untold numbers of results. Each result may yield innumerable other links, creating networks. It is these links and networks that have made shelves and organizational systems obsolete in the 2000s.

INFORMATION'S NEW PERSONALITY

Not only does information have a new look and a new home, but it also has new handlers and a new personality. It's faster, more outgoing, and more dynamic than ever before.

Information used to be produced, distributed, and managed by experts and people with money. Nineteenth-century sociologist Karl Marx noted that those who were in control of the means of production were also in control of society. The people who controlled production were also in control of the flow of information. With the arrival of digital technology, information is no longer in the hands of only a few people. This power shift allows the general public to produce and share information just as effectively as governments, businesses, and professionals. Yet this has created challenges for many information seekers. It has become increasingly important to determine the reliability of information on the Internet. College students testing the gullibility of the public can post information just as easily as scientists doing cutting-edge research.

Information also used to be hard to get. People had to leave their homes to locate a library or bookstore that had the appropriate texts. This is no longer the case. In the digital age, information can be accessed faster than ever before. In fact,

PHISHING

As more and more people moved onto digital platforms to find, share, and create information, criminals identified a new platform for their crimes. The term *phishing* entered common vocabulary in the late 1990s as a growing number of thieves began using the Internet to steal information and money from unsuspecting Internet users. Criminals "fish" for information by sending e-mails with phony links or by threatening to close or block accounts. Some phishers create sites that look like reliable websites. Unsuspecting victims type in private information, such as credit card numbers, believing they are on a familiar and trustworthy site. Those who do not take the time to verify the source and authenticity of incoming e-mails or links can easily fall prey to cybercriminals.

information often comes looking for people, as opposed to the other way around. Individuals can sign up for streams of information, such as news feeds, blogs, and social media feeds. When updates or posts are made, new information arrives on a digital platform. The information is both personalized and instantaneous, and it is delivered to people with little to no effort on the reader's part.

Another way information finds the individual is through targeted advertising. Advertisers use the Internet to collect information about user habits and interests. This allows them to selectively target their audience. While the information may be unsolicited and unwanted by the Internet user, it is nonetheless personalized.

Finally, access to information in the digital age is lightning fast. Just about any information search on the Internet will yield millions of results in a fraction of a second. Plus, with the growth

http://twitter.co

twitter

Follow you

Instant updates from yo
celebrities, and what's h

of mobile technology, individuals can find information anytime and anywhere. In addition to the speed at which information is accessible, more and more of it is available every second, and it changes constantly. Up until 1900, the amount of human knowledge doubled approximately every 100 years.[1] As of 2013, knowledge doubled every 13 months.[2] Predictions forecast that the doubling of knowledge eventually will occur every 12 hours.[3] The difficulty lies in how to identify reliable information that suits specific needs.

WHAT ABOUT THE LIBRARIANS?

Librarians are caught up in the rapid changes in information access in the digital age. Librarians were once the information gatekeepers and experts who could help researchers find the physical location of information in the

THE RISE OF MOBILE APPS

As of 2016, mobile applications, or apps, were one of the most popular ways people searched or received information about everything from the weather to games to shopping to news. Apps accounted for 52 percent of the time people spent using online media.[4] Unsurprisingly, the revenue generated by these apps continues rising; revenues increased from $35 billion to $45 billion between 2014 and 2015.[5] Apps aren't only a way for people to seek information—they are also a platform through which information finds them, in the form of push notifications. These notifications display a message on the home or lock screen even when the app is not actively in use, alerting the user to new app activity. Push notifications help to hook users so they continue using the app.

Twitter and other social media sites allow users to receive a constantly updated feed of information.

POP-UPS

Information also finds people through pop-ups. Everyone who uses the Internet has had the experience of unwanted boxes popping up on the screen. A great number of these pop-ups are designed and launched by companies trying to sell something to users. Others provide useful information, such as an alert to install or download something. There are also pop-ups that try to entice users to click on links that may ultimately download a virus onto one's computer. It is necessary to determine the legitimacy of a pop-up before acting on it. Savvy Internet users engage with pop-ups only from trusted sites.

library. Now, as information moves out of confined physical spaces, libraries and librarians are having to adapt. Public libraries, which first emerged at the beginning of the 1900s, were based on the democratic premise that information and knowledge should be free and available to anyone, no matter their ability to pay. Libraries of today continue to move forward using this same idea. Yet instead of being the traditional gatekeepers, librarians are becoming information matchmakers. Today's librarians are responsible for introducing the public to new information platforms. They also help members of the community learn important skills needed for information literacy in the digital age.

As a result, many public libraries are becoming technology hubs. The libraries themselves are places where citizens are invited to use a variety of digital tools provided by the library, including access to the Internet. For the librarian, this means helping information seekers find what they need digitally as well as on the

Today's public libraries provide members of the community with access to digital resources as well as print materials.

shelf. Librarians in schools and communities teach people how to use digital tools to efficiently find the right information. In addition, many libraries have online access to books, magazines, and other digital materials. Many are also connected to other libraries, museums, and institutions. These relationships allow a library patron to access an even broader platform of digitized information.

People still see libraries as having a critical role in the community, and many believe closing public libraries would have harmful effects. In 2015, 46 percent of people ages 16 and older

INFORMATION ADDICTION

While it may seem surprising that people can become addicted to information, there is scientific evidence backing up the claim. The pleasure systems of the human brain are controlled by dopamine, a chemical released when a person experiences gratification. It is dopamine that makes people curious about ideas and drives the search for information. In the digital age, with social media, texts, apps, and the Internet, gratification is essentially instant. That instant reward creates a drive for more gratification, which is a common phenomenon in all addictions.

reported using a library in the past 12 months.[6] Of those who did visit the library, 66 percent borrowed a print book.[7] Library patrons also use the library to study, get help from a librarian, or go on the Internet.

Other good news for librarians is that people ages 16–29 are just as likely to visit the library as are older adults. Young people use the library for both traditional and technological services. More important, 80 percent of people believe librarians are still critical in helping patrons locate the right information.[8]

> ❝ I believe public libraries should move away from being 'houses of knowledge' and move more towards being 'houses of access.' This is what the public is asking for and we are here to serve them. ❞ [9]
>
> —Librarian participant in a Pew Research Study, "Library Services in the Digital Age," 2013

Public libraries are still popular resources.

CHAPTER 4

FINDING THE CORRECT INFORMATION

Even with unlimited amounts of information available digitally, finding the correct information to fit a particular need can be challenging. Being information literate in the digital age means being aware of the diversity of digital resources, recognizing what kind of information is needed and how to search for it, and understanding how search engines and filters work.

Information seekers of the past used resources such as libraries, newspapers, phone books, and encyclopedias to find needed information. Today, most information is digitized so it can be processed easily via digital technology. In the modern world, people looking for information have all the traditional sources of information, and they also have an entire cache of digitized information. This includes everything created and shared on the Internet, which is accessible from computers, mobile phones, and tablets. Other sources of digital information include CDs, DVDs, digital cameras, and e-books. This has changed how people find information. For example, television, radio, and newspapers used

Online news sources are increasingly popular.

to be the primary source for news. But as of 2013, 50 percent of American adults reported the Internet was their main source for news.[1] For the under-30 group of adults, 71 percent report using the Internet as their news source.[2] For any information seeker, especially those doing research, the key challenge is deciding which sources to use, always keeping in mind that the information needs to be current, reliable, and accurate.

THE SEARCH

With more and more people turning to the Internet as their primary source of information, it is even more critical that searches are conducted properly. This includes being aware of how search engines work.

Boolean logic was developed in the 1800s by George Boole as a way to use logic to solve algebra problems. His goal was to link key words and phrases in order to reach mathematical conclusions. Boolean logic uses words such as *and*, *or*, and *not* to narrow or widen a set of possible results. This same logic is used by search engines. The terms used in a search will determine the type of results generated. However, not every search engine searches the same way, nor will any two search engines yield the same results. None search the entire web. Google, Yahoo, and Bing are by far the most popular and comprehensive, but there are many other search engines available for different types of searches.

Boole was a British mathematician.

Some librarians argue that starting the search process by first looking for a reliable source can lead to a more successful search. For example, an information seeker could include the name of a reliable publication in her search terms, thereby turning up any articles that publication has released on the topic of interest.

Alternately, if a specific type of information is being sought, the seeker might find more reliable information by searching within a scholarly database or a reliable website instead of conducting a general web search. For example, if an individual is seeking medical information, he could begin by searching within the Mayo Clinic website rather than using a basic search engine.

Information seekers must also be aware of search engine optimization. Commercial companies want to make sure their websites will turn up toward the top of as many search engine results as possible. Companies that hope to sell something can benefit

CONQUERING INFORMATION OVERLOAD

People are constantly bombarded with new information from numerous digital platforms. While so much information can be exciting, it can also be distracting and exhausting. Daniel Levitin, a psychology professor and the author of *The Organized Mind: Thinking Straight in the Age of Information Overload*, points out that the human brain is designed to handle only three or four things at one time. A continuous barrage of information results in overload, which causes people to lose focus and exhibit poorer judgment. It is up to the individual to decide what information is necessary for given tasks, prioritize information needs, and avoid multitasking.

by increasing the number of information seekers who encounter their website. This content might not be the best or the most reliable, but it will come up at the top of a search due to the careful search engine optimization work done as part of the company's marketing efforts. In addition to doing search engine optimization, companies can also pay a search engine to have their website show up as a sponsored link at the top of the results for a specific search.

Finally, it is also important to note that the information on the web changes every day, so information available one day may not be available the next. The information may also have changed since it was originally viewed. Of course, the more reputable the source, the more likely the information is to remain available.

HOW SEARCH ENGINES WORK

Any given search through a search engine on the Internet yields thousands, if not millions, of results in less than a second. To accomplish this, the search engine uses spiders—computer programs that crawl through the web from site to site through links, looking for key words or phrases. But search results are not actually happening in real time. Instead, the spiders, or bots, create indexes at regular intervals. Then when a search is launched, the results are actually drawn from an index created at an earlier time. The spiders are always at work. When changes are made to websites or information is added, the spiders find and index these

> " The Internet makes doing research easier . . . easier to do well and easier to do poorly. "[3]
>
> —focus group participant, Pew Research Study, 2012

changes. Due to differences in size, speed, and content, no two search engines will yield the same results. Each search engine also uses a different method for ranking search results.

THE FILTER BUBBLE

Most Internet users will find that a search engine often seems to read their mind or anticipate their search. Many search engines, including Google, tailor search results depending on past search history and user information. This means that no two researchers will end up with the same results, even if they have typed in exactly the same search terms. For example, search engines can recognize the user's current country. A search for *football* in the United States will yield results relating to American football, such as the National Football League's website. A user in Europe will end up with results about soccer. The search engine also knows the user's city or state, and often offers results that are specific to that location. The user's past searches also influence search results rankings.

> "I would actually suspect that there's more information on the Internet than there are snowflakes in a snow storm at this point. How do you search through the billions and billions of snowflakes to find the one that you are looking for? So what you need is a very fast machine that can look at every snowflake and determine, what's the snowflake I'm looking for? That's basically what search engines do."[4]
>
> —Alan Emtage

The NFL website will likely be a search result if someone in the United States searches for the term *football*.

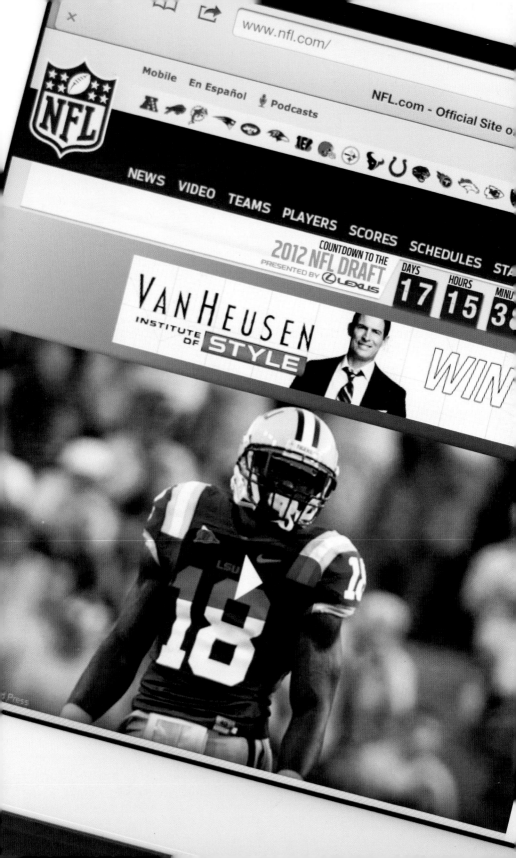

Wikipedia, the online encyclopedia that anyone, anywhere, can add to or edit, is a go-to resource for many of today's information seekers. It is also one of the Internet's most visited sites. Some people believe that this brings democracy to knowledge because anyone can create it, change it, or manipulate it. However, because Wikipedia articles are written by a variety of experts and nonexperts, the information found there cannot always be trusted. In fact, comedian Stephen Colbert called the Wikipedia phenomenon "Wikiality," in that, together, people "can create a reality that we all agree on."[6] The danger for information seekers is that there is a great deal of biased, bogus information on Wikipedia. Other Wiki editors may come along to fix errors, update information, or eliminate hoaxes. Nonetheless, information seekers should rely on Wikipedia only as a cursory introduction to a subject before seeking out more credible sources. And since individual contributors are relied upon to add content based on their own areas of interest, some experts argue that Wikipedia serves as an acceptable resource for pop culture topics, such as a TV show or movie, but should be avoided for more scholarly subjects.

These personalized search results are created by filters on the web put in place by Google, Yahoo, and even online newspapers such as the *Washington Post*. At first glance, this type of personalization seems helpful. With endless amounts of available information, receiving tailored results can save the user a great deal of time. People are shown the news and information they want. The rest is filtered out.

However, Internet activist Eli Pariser warns about living in a "filter bubble."[5] When a search engine filters search results, it shows the user what it thinks she wants to see, but it isn't showing

Pariser warns that personalized search results can prevent people from being exposed to differing points of view.

The New York Tim

CNN

World, Business, Sports, Entertainment and Video News

America   Middle East   Business

The Washington Post. Nationa

http://www.washingtonpost.com/?reload=true

The Washington Po

October 10, 2011 | In the News

www.usatoday.com/?refresh=1

News, Travel, Weather, Entertainment, Sports, Technology, U.S. &

Tim Tebow   Justice Stevens memoir

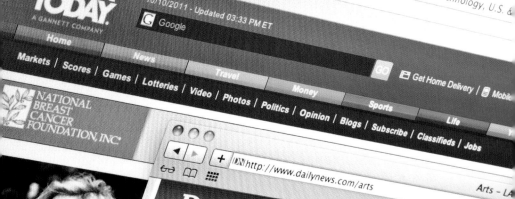

USA TODAY
A GANNETT COMPANY

10/10/2011 - Updated 03:33 PM ET

Google

Home

Markets | Scores | Games | Lotteries | Video | Photos | Politics | Opinion | Blogs | Subscribe | Classifieds | Jobs

News

Travel

Money

Sports

Life

GO   Get Home Delivery   Mobile

NATIONAL
BREAST
CANCER
FOUNDATION, INC.

DN http://www.dailynews.com/arts

Arts - LA

DailyNews
LOS ANGELES

Site   Web Search powered by YAHOO! SEARCH

Search

Home   News   Sports   Business   Opinions   Entertainment   L.A. Life   Info   Weekly A

la life the arts

Art: 'Under the Big Black Sun' exhibit reflects 'end of California Dream'

Inside the spacious Geffen Contemporary at MOCA, an
Nancy Buchanan's 1980 tribute to her nuclear physicist
occupies a wall through an assemblage of photographs,
book-bound documents and research on the important issue
of the nuclear era

rs risky for s

PHOTO

• Photo gallery: California Design

her everything. More important, it is not the user who gets to decide what she sees and what she doesn't see—it's the search engine that decides. Pariser believes people need a more balanced information diet. In a democracy, people must be able to efficiently get the relevant information they want. But it is equally important for people to be exposed to other points of view. Instead of simply assessing information that caters to their individual biases, people should also be exposed to information that challenges their beliefs or makes them feel uncomfortable.

To this end, Pariser contends part of the solution is that search engines need to be redesigned "with a sense of civic responsibility," so users—and not algorithms—get to decide what information appears on their screens.[7] The other part of the solution is increased information literacy in the digital age. By critically evaluating their sources, information seekers can be in control of the information they use and the information they leave behind.

Search engines are more likely to turn up search results from sites the user visits regularly.

AMERICANS REPORT FEELING BETTER INFORMED

On the twenty-fifth anniversary of the creation of the World Wide Web, the Pew Research Center set out to determine how Americans felt about the explosion of information available in the digital age. Rather than feeling overloaded by too much information, Americans described feeling better informed in 2014 than only five years earlier.[8] The report stated that "the vast majority of Americans believe their use of the web helps them learn new things, stay better informed on topics that matter to them, and increases their capacity to share ideas and creations with others."[9] Of the Internet users surveyed, 87 percent said they believed the Internet made it easier to learn new things.[10] This information extends to learning about products and services; local, national, and international news; popular culture; health and fitness; and even keeping up with friends and family. Of those surveyed, only 26 percent reported feeling overloaded by too much information.[11]

A majority of Americans believe the Internet makes it easier to learn new things.

CHAPTER 5

CRITICAL EVALUATION

In 2011, as tensions in Syria were mounting, the *Guardian*, the *New York Times*, Fox News, and others news media reported the kidnapping of an outspoken young Syrian woman. The woman, Amina Arraf, was well known for her blog, *Gay Girl in Damascus*. She had become an unlikely hero to many in that conservative and unstable country. Despite the constant threat of arrest by the government, Arraf continued to blog until her kidnapping. Yet it wasn't until a National Public Radio (NPR) journalist questioned her identity, wondering why he couldn't find anyone who had actually interviewed Arraf in person, that the truth emerged. Arraf simply didn't exist. A man in Scotland had created her as a means to lend credibility to his ideas and highlight the troubles in Syria.

SAVE THE PACIFIC NORTHWEST TREE OCTOPUS!

The Amina Arraf story underscores the importance of critically evaluating digital resources. Today's teachers are concerned about students' ability to judge the information they find online. Yet search engines themselves are not to blame for information failure. The responsibility lies with the information consumer.

NPR journalist Andy Carvin investigated Amina Arraf. His work led to the revelation of her real identity: a man named Tom MacMaster.

Many students report they do not believe everything they read on the Internet. But when a group of middle school students in 2006 visited a website about the critically endangered Pacific Northwest tree octopus, used as part of a literacy study, all 25 students believed the hoax.[1]

> ❝ I do not believe that I have harmed anyone—I feel that I have created an important voice for issues that I feel strongly about. ❞ [2]
> —Tom MacMaster, the man behind the Amina Arraf blog, 2012

The site itself is packed with information and looks professional. Students deemed it credible, but none of it is true.

The study was designed by Dr. Donald Leu, director of the New Literacies Research Lab at the University of Connecticut, to show that students must be taught how to evaluate the information they find online and to determine its credibility. In this case, students failed to check into who created the website. The author's personal information was falsified, including the fact that he, Lyle Zapato, went to Kelvinic University. Another quick Internet search reveals there is no such institution, leaving those interested in the tree octopus to question everything else the author reports. As with any search, this may not mean the information is false, but it does mean the information seeker must be careful. Wary Internet users must be aware that everyone with computer access can create a website or disseminate information, just as the fictitious Zapato

The University of Connecticut ran a study on information literacy using the Pacific Northwest tree octopus website.

did. Information consumers must play a game of detective to determine an author's credibility.

Another part of the detective game involves some searching about the source itself. In the tree octopus case, the information at the bottom of the home page reads, "This site is not associated with any school or educational organization, other than the Kelvinic University branch of the Wild Haggis Conservation Society."[3] Again, no such university exists. Yet there are plenty of reputable sources on the Internet. One good place to start an investigation is with a look at a site's URL suffix. The most common suffix is *.com*. This is a general suffix used by commercial sites and the general public. Other suffixes indicate a website is affiliated with certain professional organizations. For example, *.edu* is used for educational institutions, *.org* for organizations, and *.gov* for the US government. All of these suffixes are included in a search engine's search results, and those seeking information can use these suffixes to help determine the potential credibility of a source.

> " Literacy today is different from what it is going to be tomorrow because there will be a new tool, a new technology that'll be available for us. "[4]
>
> —Dr. Donald Leu, 2014

Scholarly databases are some of the most credible sources of information on the web. These databases are collections of information for academic purposes, including journal articles on specific areas of study. These sources are highly reliable because the information there is all reviewed by peers, or other professionals in the same field.

Nonprofessionals are not always poor sources of information. But evaluating the authority of the website's author helps the researcher determine the usefulness of the source, as well as its potential bias and its origins. The researcher must also recognize that different types of information require different levels of authority. For example, when looking for the latest research on addictions, it is important to find information from an expert such as a psychologist or doctor. However, when seeking reviews on a band's most recent concert, reliable information could come from an online community of fans. The key to determining the level of authority required is to understand the type of information needed and how it will be used.

CONTENT EVALUATION

Environmentalists and octopus lovers alike may be prone to buy into the hoax of the Pacific Northwest tree octopus. After all, the article is full of scientific-sounding facts and authentic-looking photographs. But all of that information comes from an unreliable source. Information seekers must also be fact-checkers and use the abundance of information available on the Internet to their advantage. It is easy enough to surf from site to site and link to link to make sure facts and claims on one website hold up on others. A quick Internet search on the tree octopus reveals the creature never existed. The case of the fictitious tree octopus also shows how important it is to check multiple sources when seeking information, no matter whether you're researching an endangered species or looking for a good place to eat.

Likewise, it is true that websites should be evaluated for their bias. Even if the author or the site's affiliated organization is credible, the content on the page may be biased, or present a specific point of view. Political websites provide excellent examples of content with bias because they present only one side of political issues. Furthermore, the opinions expressed on such sites are stated as if they are fact. They often do not acknowledge the other side of an argument. Similarly, when reading other websites or articles, one can suspect bias if only one side of an issue is presented. Bias should also be suspected if the authors or contributors all have similar affiliations, or if the tone is

Information from political websites, such as the Drudge Report, may be biased toward a specific political viewpoint.

OBAMA TURNS TO CONGRESS...
Seeks Authorization for Syria Strike...
Change of heart after taking walk...
Krauthammer: 'Amateur Hour'...
House, Senate to hold hearings next week...
President risks embarrassing loss...
Leaves door open if Congress votes 'no'...
Hollande facing pressure to put intervention to vote...

FINGER ON THE TRIGGER PAUSES

DRUDGE REPORT

Syria Faces Cyber Attacks in Upcoming Strikes...

U.S. Had Intel on Chemical Strike Before It Was Launched...

'UTTER NONSENSE'

Egypt detains swan for suspected spying...

Massive Yosemite blaze may have been sparked by illegal marijuana growers...

Supreme Court Justice to officiate same-sex wedding...

Summer of 2013 among coolest on record in Alabama...

Man accused of threatening 'to behead' Congresswoman arrested in Mexico...

SHOCK: Wife boils husband in pressure cooker...

Justin Timberlake Wants to Play the Riddler in 'BATMAN'...

Husband, Wife Married 71 Years Die 16 Hours Apart...

PATRIOTS RELEASE TEBOW...

Cornel West: MLK 50 Was 'Coronation of Bonafide House Negro of Obama Plantation... Al Sharpton'...

REPORT: NSA Hacked AL JAZEERA...

Snowden wins whistleblower award in Germany...

Test Reveals Tech Giants Snooping on Emails...

MICROSOFTGOOGLE to sue over surveillance requests...

Police storm homeschool class, take children by force...

COPS: 2 Women Gang Raped By Group Of 10-12 Juveniles In Park... Developing...

Three teens charged with sports camp sex assaults...

No Atlantic Hurricane by August in First Time in 11 Years...

Pope breaks protocol by bowing to Queen of Jordan...

First papal 'selfie' goes viral...

COPS: Teen Attacks, Robs 82-Year-Old Woman Leaving Church After Sunday Mass...

Cruz showered with praise at tea party summit...

'Run, Ted, run!'...

Iowa Democrat prayer: Thank God for abortions!

5-Year-Old Getting Medical Marijuana Card...

Pop Group Beating 'BUTLER' at Boxoffice... Developing...

Hollywood Rehab Center Closes After Two Deaths...

Bieber attacked in Toronto nightclub...

COURT ALLOWS OBAMA TO KEEP WHITE HOUSE VISITOR LOGS SECRET...

Sealed for up to 12 years...

Rand Paul: Boehner speakership in jeopardy over immigration...

Rubio Heckled...

...declines to discuss bill during event

Air National Guard Accidentally Drops 'Practice' Bomb Into Bar Parking Lot...

GET IT ON THE GO: DRUDGE IPHONE/IPAD APP...

AGENCE FRANCE-PRESSE
AFP NEWS WRAP
REUTERS WORLD NEWS HIGHLIGHTS
REUTERS DIGEST
REUTERS WORLD
REUTERS POLITICS
REUTERS ODD

◀   ▶   ⬆   📖   7

emotional. A neutral website or article will state facts, use data, and objectively examine both sides of an issue.

This is where the personalization of search filters becomes troublesome. Information seekers often get only the information the search engine thinks they want. Users need to seek out multiple viewpoints on a subject from a variety of sources in order to be well informed. This type of thinking also forces information seekers to confront their own beliefs and to challenge the beliefs of others.

DECONSTRUCTING MEDIA MESSAGES

Critical evaluation can also help uncover the untold messages in advertisements—the subtext that is unspoken or unseen, yet is there just the same. This can include propagating stereotypes or using various marketing techniques to target specific consumers and make them want to buy a product. For example, an ad campaign for Reese's Puffs cereal features teens eating the cereal while grooving to hip-hop music in bright and colorful settings, yet it never refers to the cereal's nutritional content. The underlying message is that everyone's morning can be fun if they eat Reese's Puffs. Other ad campaigns use celebrities to sell their products. Some rely on the bandwagon technique, which is designed to get consumers to believe that "everyone" is using a certain product so that consumers will purchase the product to avoid feeling left out. With every advertisement, consumers need to be aware of the marketing techniques being used, as well as the bias of the advertiser—to get people to buy its product.

Ad campaigns frequently use celebrities to sell their products, such as in this 2013 Pepsi ad campaign featuring Beyoncé Knowles.

Finally, sources must also be evaluated to determine how recently the information was posted. In an age when information is added and updated constantly, getting the most current information is important. Similarly, old information on the Internet never dies, and it may appear as one of the top ten search results just as easily as new information. Finding a publication date can

ART OR DECEPTION?

The ease of digital image editing has raised a debate between photojournalists, artists, and everyday information seekers about how much manipulation is ethical. With digital tools, photographers can easily add, subtract, filter, enhance, straighten, crop, sharpen, and tone their images. Some say this is photo manipulation in the name of art. Others say it is cheating. They believe that photographers should be trusted to tell the truth with their images, especially in journalism. A research study on "The Integrity of the Image" was conducted in 2014. It found that, at least with respect to photojournalism, image manipulation (adding or subtracting elements with the intent of misleading) is unacceptable. However, adjustments (cropping, toning, adjusting color, or other similar techniques) are accepted if they are minor.

be a challenge, but it is crucial to getting reliable and current information. For example, using information about the planets of the solar system posted before 2006 will result in incorrect information; Pluto was reclassified as a dwarf planet in 2006, leaving just eight planets in the solar system, not nine. For this reason, information seekers must carefully evaluate their sources before making use of any information.

A photographer who edited a video camera out of his 2013 image of a Syrian opposition fighter got into trouble for violating the ethics of photojournalism.

CHAPTER 6

LEARNING HOW TO SHARE IN THE DIGITAL AGE

One of the most powerful aspects of digital technology is that it has allowed people to move from being passive consumers of information to interactive producers. Thanks to information and communication technology, users can study together, collaborate, share information, build communities, and access resources. In this virtual workspace, students can learn from online courses. Businesses can operate with employees located all over the world. Not only can people work together and have creative conversations, but they can also learn from each other. This ease of communication allows new opportunities for innovation and creative problem solving.

CONTROL OF INFORMATION

Digital technology has become a democratizing force in the 2000s, allowing anyone with Internet access the ability to share information with the world. Information is no longer shared from the top down, but from everyday people around the world. Books are no longer published only by large publishing houses, and

Using recent technology, it is now easier for businesses to operate with employees located in many different places.

news is no longer reported solely by formal news organizations. Information does not flow in only one direction anymore. Today's information consumers are connected to each other, which allows them to take on the role of information producer.

In 2008, this new role played a major part in the spread of news about a massive earthquake in China's Sichuan Province. China has a long history of filtering information before it reaches its citizens. While digital technology continues to advance at a rapid rate, the Chinese government carefully monitors what information reaches the Chinese public. This is called the Great Firewall of China. Yet this firewall only filters the information coming into China. It does not police what information goes out. The Chinese government was caught off guard during the destructive earthquake. Chinese citizens reported the quake as it happened, immediately sending out videos, photos, and tweets to the rest of the world. Government officials actually heard about the quake from ordinary people experiencing it firsthand, rather than from their own censored news organization. The news went worldwide before they could do anything.

> "The most useful impact is the ability to connect people. From that, everything flows."[1]
>
> —Dan Lynch, founder of Interop and former director of computing facilities at SRI International, 2014

At first the government decided to let the citizen reporting continue. But then citizens also began to report that the reason so many schools had collapsed during the quake, killing many students and teachers, was that corrupt officials had taken bribes

Survivors light incense in memory of victims of China's 2008 earthquake. News about the quake spread quickly through social media.

to allow the construction of subpar buildings. That spurred the government to shut down entire communication services. But the information was already out there, produced in real time by real people and available anywhere in the world.

THE POWER OF THE NETWORK

The 2008 earthquake in China demonstrated the power of social networks on the Internet and showed how these digital networks have become an integral part of the lives of millions of people. Users can create networks of friends, family, or colleagues. There are blogs, forums, social and professional networking sites, message boards, photo-sharing sites, e-commerce platforms, and more, and all of these platforms serve to create connections between individuals. The ways in which these networks can be harnessed is limited only by the human imagination.

Social networks also have power to influence ideas, relationships, behavior, health, and politics in the real world. Social media is also effectively used to raise awareness, or to rally support for individuals or groups. The It Gets Better Project is a powerful example of how social media can rally people. The campaign was launched in September 2010 by author Dan Savage and his husband, Terry Miller, in response to the increasing number of suicides by teens who were the targets of bullying because of their sexual orientation. The video the duo created was meant to show teens that life does, in fact, get better. Since its release, the video has been viewed more than two million times. In addition, 50,000 other videos with messages of hope have been added by individuals, and those videos have been viewed more than 50 million times.[2]

Dan Savage, *right*, and his husband, Terry Miller, were granted the Governors Award at the 2015 Creative Arts Emmys for the It Gets Better Project.

HYPERCONNECTIVITY

Hyperconnectivity in the digital age means that everything and everyone is talking to one another and sharing information: people are talking to people, machines are talking to machines, and people and machines are talking to each other. This hyperconnectivity holds the power to solve problems and generate innovation in all aspects of the modern world, because it creates, stores, and shares data across networks. For example, the energy industry currently uses hyperconnected networks to predict and therefore prevent power outages, or to reroute power in order to maximize efficiency. In health care, hyperconnectivity allows real-time monitoring of patients even when they are not in the hospital. This allows doctors to react instantly to patient needs, ultimately saving lives. Software engineer Vivek Ranadivé, whose software company works with real-time technology believes, "If you get the right information to the right place at the right time and in the right context, you can make the world a better place."[3]

THE INTERCONNECTED WORLD

Interconnectedness has reshaped the definition of information literacy. Information literacy in this environment requires that people not only seek, retrieve, and evaluate information, but also actively participate, create, and interact. Internet users need to be aware of how social networks work and evolve. For example, many social networks have their own filters that alter the type of information people receive. This makes critically evaluating sources of information even more important.

> "Facebook is a powerful tool, but that's because, at its core, it connects real friends."[4]
>
> —James Fowler, author and University of California, San Diego, professor, 2013

While the Internet can be a powerful tool, information literacy requires users to be aware of the bubbles created by these filters and by their own social connections. Social networks allow users to connect with people who share similar beliefs and values. While being surrounded by like-minded people can be comforting, it is important to remember that opposing ideas and opinions are often hidden outside the bubble. Social networks such as Facebook continually feed members personalized information and connections. It can be argued that this type of personalization is simply a digital reflection of the connections made in the real world. It is also a way to work around the massive amounts of information that exist. However, users need to be aware of the biases these filters introduce.

Furthermore, Internet users need to be aware of the potential consequences

VISUAL STORYTELLING

Marketing professionals love the digital age because technology allows them to share more information quickly and efficiently. However, in an age when consumers are confronted daily with untold numbers of images, marketers must create visual stories that have an impact. This strategy uses images and videos on social media to tell customers a visual story about their product. The NFL's New England Patriots even used visual storytelling as a way to keep fans passionate about their team in the off-season. During a massive February 2013 snowstorm, the team used Facebook to post one album of past games played in the snow and another album featuring snowmen wearing Patriots jerseys. The story allowed fans to engage with the team, and reminded them to buy Patriots merchandise.

facebook   Home   Profile

View Photos of Mark

View Videos of Mark

Send Mark a Message

Poke Mark

Information

Networks:
Harvard
Facebook

Relationship Status:
In a relationship with
Priscilla Chan

of reposting, retweeting, or sharing information online. Not only can these actions reinforce biases within one's online community, but they can also perpetuate the spread of misinformation. For example, during the Ebola outbreak in Africa in 2014, social media posts fueled rumors the epidemic had spread to the United States and was running rampant in US cities. In addition, the rumors falsely reported how Ebola is spread. The key to containing the spread of misinformation in the virtual world is to verify information before passing it along.

VIRAL VIDEOS

The power of social networks is demonstrated by online videos that go viral. First, a video is posted, then someone likes it or shares it with their social network, then those people share it in their network. People may continue sharing the video in this way until it has been seen by thousands or millions of people. Yet most videos do not get millions of hits. The success of a video depends on people known as tastemakers. These are people whose opinions about current cultural trends influence the opinions of others. Ultimately these tastemakers help determine what information is perceived as important. When a tastemaker tweets, links, likes, blogs, or shares a particular video, more people are drawn to it. People are also drawn to videos that are unexpected or unusual, or those that allow for creative participation.

Facebook CEO Mark Zuckerberg discusses his popular social media platform at a conference in 2011.

THE ALS ICE BUCKET CHALLENGE

In the summer of 2014, videos of people enduring large buckets of ice poured over their heads were splashed across social media. This "ice bucket challenge" was initiated as a general charity fund-raising campaign. The idea was that one person would nominate another person to either donate to a charity or take on the challenge and record videos of themselves being doused—or both. Regardless of how they chose to participate, people used social media to spread information about the ice bucket challenge in an effort to raise awareness and to promote fund-raising for charity.

The challenge was eventually linked with ALS (also known as Lou Gehrig's disease), a degenerative disease that attacks the brain and spinal cord. Then when two men, Pat Quinn and Pete Frates, who both have ALS, promoted the challenge using social media, the videos began to go viral. Frates is especially credited with the explosion on social media due to his extensive online social networks. By leveraging social networks, participants in the challenge made ALS a household word within a matter of weeks.

Many celebrities participated in the ALS ice bucket challenge. Heidi Klum, *left*, dumped ice on Tim Gunn during the season finale of *Project Runway* in 2014.

The ALS Association initially had no knowledge of the challenge. That changed in late July 2014, when it noticed a significant increase in donations. In less than two months, the organization received $114 million in donations, as compared to $5 million in the same time period the year before.[5] Likewise, increasing numbers of people had begun to follow the ALS Association on social media sites and to visit the ALS Association website. While the organization did not start the ice bucket challenge, it is now a central part of its website.

CHAPTER 7

ETHICS AND RESPONSIBILITY

Being a good Internet user comes with certain responsibilities and social expectations, which are all part of being information literate in the digital age. These responsibilities include respect for others on the Internet, being safe, remaining ethical, thinking before clicking, being aware of what one shares on the Internet, and understanding actions in the virtual world can and do have real world consequences.

FAIR USE ON A DIGITAL PLATFORM

Almost half of Americans today participate in online piracy. That number is even higher among adults under 30, at 70 percent.[1] But it is illegal to download, share, or copy unauthorized music, books, movies, TV shows, and other digital media. These are all forms of stealing. Yet many people think passing along the latest movie or song between friends is harmless, and the likelihood of getting caught is extremely small. This attitude has led to a copy culture.

When the Internet was gaining popularity in the early 1990s, no one predicted how common online piracy would become. The first case to reach national headlines involved a service called

The Martian, a film starring Matt Damon, was a frequent victim of online piracy in 2015.

NAPSTER'S LEGACY

While much of the press over Napster's free download service focused on the illegality and the lawsuit that ultimately forced the service's shutdown and payments to musicians, some coverage also heralded a new era of music distribution and consumption. For many music lovers it was the first time they could easily find access to obscure or out-of-date music. Further, the era of having to buy an entire album just to get one or two tracks was over. And while many professional musicians believed they should be compensated for each download, amateur artists were grateful for the new platform. It was a way to get their music out to the public and receive feedback in return. These new musicians were no longer at the mercy of big label recording companies. Since Napster's rise and fall, file sharing on the Internet has continued to evolve, and the issues around it have yet to be resolved.

Napster, which allowed anyone with an Internet connection to download music for free. The company was started on June 1, 1999, by teenagers Shawn Fanning and Sean Parker. By the middle of 2000, Napster had more than 20 million users.[2] Yet it had also stirred up a frenzy of irate musicians and a fiery debate in the music industry that was to be the first of its kind about online piracy. Many in the industry felt as if Fanning and Parker were thieves, depriving musicians of money they had rightfully earned, while music lovers everywhere thought of them as heroes. The issue was that the digital platform for sharing information was so new, and changing so quickly, that Napster's idea challenged

Napster cofounder Sean Parker gives a talk at the Web 2.0 Conference in 2011.

existing social norms and forced a debate over copyright and intellectual property rights in the digital era.

Copyright laws were originally put in place to protect and compensate content creators for their work. The laws were also meant to give creators some measure of control over how their work was used. Debates over what constitutes fair use and plagiarism are not new. But what is new is that in the digital era, making perfect copies of information is both cheap and fast. Yet just because information is found on the Internet does not mean that it is free or that there isn't a victim. The reality is that the creator has had his or her work stolen.

In the current copy culture, there is further debate about copying and sharing digital media among friends and family (which many people see as harmless) versus making copies for widespread public use. There is also debate over the extent to which users should be monitored for pirated material. Unfortunately, copyright laws

COPYRIGHT ORIGINS

The history of copyright laws in the United States dates back to the drafting of the US Constitution. The force behind the copyright clause was Noah Webster, of Webster's dictionaries, as he campaigned for the inclusion of the laws in the 1780s. The clause grants Congress the power "to promote the progress of science and useful arts, by securing for limited times to authors and inventors the exclusive right to their respective writings and discoveries.[3] Advocates for the clause, including Webster, believed that such a law would ensure authors were paid for their work, which would, in turn, help generate American literature and foster creativity. The Copyright Act became part of the Constitution in 1790.

US legislators are still debating how to crack down on online piracy. In 2011, two bills were proposed to address the issue: the Stop Online Piracy Act (SOPA) and the Protect Intellectual Property Act (PIPA). The goal was to end the theft of music and films from online platforms, targeting those hosted on foreign servers. Yet United States–based Internet providers were concerned they could be held responsible for illegal content shared by users if they failed to remove content or disable websites.

While some supported the bills, many feared SOPA and PIPA would restrict Internet freedom and lead to censorship. On January 18, 2012, hundreds of websites, including Wikipedia, shut down in protest. Google put a black censorship bar across its logo and collected digital signatures from seven million people in protest. The bills never moved forward. As of 2016, there was still talk among legislators about updating copyright laws, but no new measures had been passed.

about information on the Internet have yet to catch up to the speed with which the Internet is changing and growing.

> Bottom line: Artists should be compensated for the music they make. It's that simple. [4]
>
> —LL Cool J, hip-hop artist

INTERNET ABUSE

Using the Internet to pirate digital media is not the only way people abuse the Internet. One of the most serious examples of Internet abuse involves online bullying, or cyberbullying. Bullies existed long before the Internet, but digital tools have given them a new environment in which to harass their victims 24 hours a day, seven days a week. Victims are no longer safe within their own homes, but are subjected to hateful messages and images online. Worse, if the information is shared on the Internet, it can reach a vast

audience very quickly while the bully often stays anonymous. The impact on victims is overwhelming, and an increasing number of cyberbullying victims have committed suicide due to the relentless attacks.

These types of headlines, and the overall number of cyberbullying cases, have increased as Internet usage has risen. Yet just as with copyright laws, cyberbullying laws are still playing catch-up. In fact, as of 2015, all 50 states and the District of Columbia had antibullying laws, but only 22 included cyberbullying.[5]

In the digital age, information literacy requires people to understand the legal and social issues involved in Internet use so they can participate responsibly and ethically. This means not only understanding copyright and fair use issues, but also respecting the rights of others.

> ❝ Cyberbullying is poised to turn into the biggest online concern, already affecting up to 35 percent of all children. ❞ [6]
>
> —Dr. Martyn Wild, expert on cybersafety

Tina Meier, whose 13-year-old daughter Megan committed suicide after experiencing cyberbullying, speaks about online safety to a small group of students.

CHAPTER 8

SIGNIFICANT EFFECTS OF TECHNOLOGY

Digital technology has transformed the way people seek, find, use, share, and create knowledge. And with this change, there has been a fundamental shift in how people learn and how schools teach.

DEMOCRATIZATION

Perhaps the single greatest effect of digital technology, and specifically mobile technology, is that information can be made available to anyone, anywhere on the globe. Even in developing countries, which historically have had limited information technology, recent years have brought an era of widespread mobile digital tools. And in the United States, even though computers and Internet access are not available in every home, an increasing number of students have mobile phones. Similarly, a growing percentage of students have access to the Internet and mobile technology in school and community libraries.

This democratization of information has the power to change education. Many schools are able to provide more personalized

A student at a public school in Villa Cardal, Uruguay, learns how to use a laptop that was provided by the One Laptop Per Child project.

Language instruction in schools is expensive. It requires both specialized materials and teachers who are fluent in the language. Remote locations and developing nations have difficulty attracting qualified teachers. In some schools, robots are now being used for language instruction. Because of the nature of language acquisition, which involves memorization and repetition, robots are ideal substitute teachers.

In South Korea, some students are taught English from one of two robots—Engkey or MERO. Engkey gets its name from "English Disc Jockey." It can move around and is able to interact with students. MERO is only a head, but it is just as good at teaching English. Children had positive responses to working with the robots and have experienced increased motivation to learn English. While the overall results in language acquisition were mixed, the robots nonetheless filled an educational need and had a positive impact in the classrooms.

learning that is facilitated by digital tools. This is a blessing for teachers and students alike, since classrooms generally contain a diverse group of learners with varying skills and interests. Personalized digital content and personalized learning environments can customize learning for each individual in the classroom. Digital technology also has the ability to provide ongoing feedback and assessments.

Students with learning disabilities can be especially well served by digital technology. This population of learners is often underserved due to a lack of resources, and overextended teachers can sometimes find it challenging to provide the individualized attention the students require. For these students, learning

A student with a hearing disability uses an iPad to learn.

is frequently frustrating. With technology, however, teachers can effectively respond to student needs and personalize their education, allowing for student success and engagement. At a special-needs school in Japan, for example, teachers use different apps for each student, depending on what the student needs. Not only that, the simplicity of touching and dragging icons on a tablet allows for students with motor issues to be able to complete tasks. At a similar school in New York, a young man was completely nonverbal until his teachers gave him an iPad. The device had a communication app on it, allowing the student to begin communicating with words. The tool also inspired him to try to use his own voice for the first time.

EMPHASIS ON INFORMATION LITERACY SKILLS OVER KNOWLEDGE

With technology transforming education, information literacy today emphasizes learning the necessary skills to navigate the digital world effectively and appropriately. To this end, teachers in the digital age are not suppliers of knowledge but of skills. Students have less need to memorize facts. Instead, they need to know how to find and evaluate the facts.

Because of this, students are moving toward a more inquiry-based education and are asked to approach their own investigations and research by asking critical questions. As a result, students must take more active roles in their own learning. This approach builds skills that carry over into adulthood.

Tablets have become increasingly popular classroom tools.

CONSTANT ENGAGEMENT

Digital technology has reduced the need for time-consuming memorization and given students new platforms on which to engage in their own learning. Teachers report that digital technology, while sometimes a distraction, has a positive impact on student motivation. Students themselves report their own positive engagement with learning technologies.

In addition, online platforms facilitate ongoing classroom discussions, giving all students a voice. They also allow students to collaborate outside the classroom without being in the same physical space, ask questions about assignments, and get support from teachers and peers. In this manner, technology extends learning beyond the classroom

NO MORE BOOK REPORTS!

In one high school English class in Kansas, teacher Brandi McWilliams did away with traditional book reports. She found that such reports usually began with, "This book is about . . ." but didn't require any interaction or deep thought about a book on the part of the student. Now, using iPads, students can create a soundtrack for scenes in classic novels using the GarageBand app. In addition, students are required to write a paper explaining how their soundtrack relates to the literature. McWilliams believes digital technology facilitates passion and deeper learning: "They don't just memorize the book and spit it back out for me. They know it because they're involved in it; they're visualizing it. This kind of project took their thinking to another level."[1]

Technology allows students to connect with teachers and peers even after they've left the classroom.

walls. Learning is no longer limited to school hours within school buildings—it is an ongoing process.

MOOCS

The term *MOOC*, which stands for Massive Open Online Course, was coined in 2008 when George Siemens and Stephen Downes offered a free course in partnership with the University of Manitoba. Classes are taught online, where students and professors interact on various online platforms. Unlike traditional classrooms, MOOCs can educate thousands of students at one time. In addition, the classes are open to anyone, anywhere. There is no admission process, and the classes are free. While there is discussion about some fees for MOOCs in the future, the prediction is that they will be minimal, nothing like the cost of college tuition in the United States. Experts predict MOOCs are setting the groundwork for changes in higher education, thus allowing opportunities for everyone and democratizing knowledge.

Digital engagement also gives students real-time connections to the real world. Students, no longer having to rely on print media, have access to the latest information anywhere in the world. In this way, the world is brought into the classroom or home as it changes and evolves. Just as important, students no longer receive information passively. Instead they can create their own information to share with others worldwide by contributing to online debates, movements, and other social platforms. This type of engagement empowers students as they become a part of real-world events. And where traditional methods of teaching generally only allow work to be seen by teachers or peers in

DIGITAL LEARNING EQUITY ACT

One of the main efforts of the American Library Association is to support equal access to information. Technology has provided new educational opportunities for many people, but not everyone has equal access to this technology. The American Library Association works to ensure everyone has access to the information they need in a variety of formats, regardless of the person's age, race, gender, religion, or any other factor. To address this equity gap, it is important that all libraries are equipped with the technology and resources kids need to succeed. To this end, the Digital Learning Equity Act was introduced to a congressional committee in September 2015 in an effort to broaden access for millions of students and to make use of the role that libraries play in communities both now and in the future.

a classroom, the Internet also allows students to share their work with a larger audience.

> The biggest impact on the world will be universal access to all human knowledge. The smartest person in the world currently could well be stuck behind a plow in India or China. Enabling that person—and the millions like him or her—will have a profound impact on the development of the human race. [2]
>
> —Hal Varian, chief economist for Google

Students must participate in this real-world digital platform with an informed mind, and it is here that information literacy is especially important. Applied and used effectively and ethically, digital technology can have transformative effects that reach around the world and into the future, changing lives for the better.

CHAPTER 9

THE FUTURE OF LITERACY

In 2003, before the explosion of social media and online communities, literacy experts from around the world met and identified the need to expand on the traditional definition of information literacy to include digital platforms. They met in Prague, Czech Republic, and issued *The Prague Declaration: "Towards an Information Literate Society,"* which addressed the importance of growing information and communication technologies in information literacy. More important, the document highlighted the need for "an integrated approach to information literacy that considers the interrelationships between information, communication, and technology."[1] It also stated information literacy is a fundamental human right.

DIRECT INFORMATION LITERACY INSTRUCTION

In a study released in 2012, teachers rated student research skills as poor even though their students were digital natives. In addition, teachers reported more than 50 percent of their students were "fair" or "poor" at assessing the quality of online information,

Literacy experts agree technology plays an increasingly important role in teaching information literacy.

recognizing bias in online content, and having patience in finding the right information.[2]

This is where digital media literacy and information literacy converge. Both types of literacy allow people to be informed users of digital media and information and successfully create and share their own messages. Therefore, in order for students to be able to critically evaluate websites, such as that of the Pacific Northwest tree octopus, these skills must be taught at the same time. Yet the grade at which to begin digital media literacy, and who should teach it, is still up for debate. These decisions vary by school and school district. Some teachers see the need for information literacy in the digital age to start in elementary school, while others believe that middle or high school is a good age to start. Some schools rely on the English department to teach these skills, while others expect all teachers in a building to teach and reinforce these skills with the help of library staff. Teachers agree class time should be devoted to direct instruction and application of information literacy skills, and assignments should require students to use their new media and information literacy skills.

Despite the lack of central education guidelines regarding information and digital media literacy in the United States, many teachers are implementing their own lessons that address the interaction between these literacies. For example, Dr. Craig Roble teaches middle school social studies in Minnesota. In order to engage his students in history, he uses digital media to create

Information literacy skills can be incorporated into a variety of class subjects.

an interactive textbook, using videos, images, and web links to enliven history that would otherwise be inaccessible to his students. Not only are students in Roble's classroom improving their information literacy skills, but they are also improving their digital media literacy.

REPERCUSSIONS OF ILLITERACY

Illiteracy has individual, social, and economic effects that impact everyone. For example, 60 percent of the prison population cannot read; 85 percent of juvenile offenders also have reading difficulties.[3] In fact, when some states make predictions about future numbers of prison beds, they look at reading scores of current elementary school students. Furthermore, 75 percent of individuals receiving welfare cannot read.[4] Not only does illiteracy impact an individual's ability to succeed, but, as a whole, it has a staggeringly negative impact on the economy as more social services and prison spaces are needed.

> "Students have told me the biggest difference in the way they're learning is that they're active. They're participating. . . . It helps sustain their mental effort and their interest."[5]
>
> —Dr. Craig Roble, middle school social studies teacher, talking about using iPads in the classroom

The correlations cannot be ignored, nor can the broader implications for a functioning, flourishing democracy. In fact, in a 2013 international survey of literacy rates in advanced economies, the United States ranked fifteenth out of 23.[6]

Harry Potter author J. K. Rowling presents achievement certificates to inmates in Edinburgh Prison who have learned to read through a prison literacy program.

One way to combat illiteracy is to close the digital divide. Governments, communities, libraries, and schools must work together to ensure everyone has access to the Internet and digital tools. Leaders are increasingly recognizing the disparities in access, and since 2009 the US government has installed or upgraded more than 100,000 miles (161,000 km) of Internet infrastructure, providing broadband Internet connections to 45 million more Americans.[7] President Obama's goal also includes high-speed broadband connections in 99 percent of US classrooms by 2018.[8]

INFORMATION LITERACY IN THE WORKFORCE

In 2014, Project Information Literacy funded an annual survey of employers, and a common theme emerged: the lack of basic research skills among recent college graduates. Surprising numbers of college graduates who had grown up in the digital age lacked traditional skills in both research and analysis.[9] Potential employers found these job candidates to be tech savvy, yet mired in the information surplus. Another survey by Project Information Literacy found that students were unable to effectively sort through information, find the right information, and determine authenticity.[10]

A wireless broadband technician tests equipment at the top of a 75-foot (23 m) tower in South Hero, Vermont.

Between November 2013 and January 2014, a group of technology experts was asked to make predictions about digital life in the year 2025. They agreed the world would continue to change quickly, with individuals increasingly connected to a steady stream of information. They felt this would have both positive and negative consequences. Some of the positive predictions included the idea that the Internet will flow through people's lives as effortlessly as electricity, that global connectivity will increase as the Internet continues to grow, and that the world will operate on a completely connected system of mobile and wearable technology.

However, the predictions were not all positive. Some experts warned about an ever-increasing digital divide, putting those without digital tools at a greater disadvantage. Abuse of the Internet, in forms such as theft, stalking, and bullying, was also predicted to increase.

INFORMATION LITERACY = OPPORTUNITY

Literacy is just as important as it always has been. People need to be able to read, write, and access information. And while information has undergone an enormous transformation, it is still information. Understanding how to evaluate the credibility, relevance, reliability, and timeliness of information is just as important as it has always been. Libraries and librarians remain a valuable source for information resources. Really, the only things that have changed are the platform and the amount of information available.

Part of being information literate today is taking responsibility for the information one consumes. Information consumers must not always rely on information that is free and easy to access. They should take the time to look for information that may be difficult to find or uncomfortable to learn. People must also be able to use expanding digital technology to find, evaluate, create, and share information. As the American Library Association Presidential Committee on Information Literacy reported in 1989:

> *Ultimately, information literate people are those who have learned how to learn. They know how to learn because they know how knowledge is organized, how to find information, and how to use information in such a way that others can learn from them. They are people prepared for lifelong learning, because they can always find the information needed for any task or decision at hand.*[11]

It is this combination of skills that will offer information literate people intellectual, monetary, and social advantages.

Information literacy is a powerful and important set of skills. At their core, these skills allow individuals to be effective when consuming information and when communicating ideas. Those who are information literate in the digital age have countless opportunities before them.

> " Today high speed broadband is not a luxury, it's a necessity. "[12]
>
> —President Obama, January 14, 2015

ESSENTIAL FACTS

MAJOR EVENTS

» On January 10, 1989, the Presidential Committee on Information Literacy released a report about the changing nature of education and information in the digital age.

» In 1990, college student Alan Emtage created Archie, the world's first search engine.

» In 1991, the National Literacy Act of 1991 was passed in order to promote literacy in the Information Age.

» On October 1, 2009, President Barack Obama declared October National Information Literacy Awareness Month.

» Between 2011 and 2013, 90 percent of the information in the world was created.

KEY PLAYERS

» George Boole developed Boolean logic, which linked key words and phrases to more efficiently guide queries; his method is the same one used by Internet search engines today.

» Alan Emtage created the very first search engine.

» Eli Pariser, Internet activist, warned Internet users about living in a filter bubble.

» Kyle Stoneman created Gullible.info, a social experiment to show people's willingness to believe what they read on the Internet.

IMPACT ON SOCIETY

Today anyone, anywhere in the world can access, evaluate, use, share, create, and communicate information instantly with networks of other individuals around the globe. With this explosion of knowledge comes the need for new information literacy skills. These new skills include not only digital literacy and the ability to use technology efficiently, but also the critical thinking skills necessary to access, evaluate, and use information effectively and ethically.

QUOTE

"Ultimately, information literate people are those who have learned how to learn. They know how to learn because they know how knowledge is organized, how to find information, and how to use information in such a way that others can learn from them. They are people prepared for lifelong learning, because they can always find the information needed for any task or decision at hand."

—American Library Association Presidential Committee on Information Literacy, January 10, 1989

GLOSSARY

ALGORITHM
A set of steps that can be coded into a computer program to complete a process.

CYBERBULLYING
The use of the Internet to bully or harass, including sending intimidating messages, posting unwanted photos and videos, or creating false profiles.

CYBERCRIMINAL
A person who uses electronic devices to commit an illegal activity, such as accessing private information.

DIGITAL NATIVE
A person born or brought up during the digital age.

DIGITIZE
To put information into digital form.

FAIR USE
The limited use of some copyrighted material without the permission of the creator.

FIREWALL
Computer hardware or software that blocks unauthorized users.

PATENT

To obtain a legal document giving the inventor sole rights to manufacture or sell a physical item.

PIRACY

The act of illegally using someone's product, invention, or idea.

PLAGIARISM

The act of copying and claiming another person's words or ideas as your own.

SEARCH ENGINE

A computer program used to search for information on the Internet using key words and phrases.

SOCIOECONOMIC

Related to both social and economic factors.

VIRUS

A computer program that performs a harmful action, such as destroying information.

ADDITIONAL RESOURCES

SELECTED BIBLIOGRAPHY

Harris, Frances Jacobson. *I Found It on the Internet*. Chicago: American Library Association, 2011. Print.

Mackey, Thomas P. and Trudi E. Jacobson. *Metaliteracy: Reinventing Information Literacy to Empower Learners*. Chicago: American Library Association, 2014. Print.

Pahomov, Larissa. *Authentic Learning in the Digital Age: Engaging Students Through Inquiry*. Alexandria, VA: ASCD, 2014. Print.

Seife, Charles. *Virtual Unreality*. New York: Viking/The Penguin Group, 2014. Print.

FURTHER READINGS

Endsley, Kezia. *How to Do Great Online Research*. New York: Cavendish, 2015. Print.

Patchin, Justin W. and Sameer Hinduja. *Words Wound: Delete Cyberbullying and Make Kindness Go Viral*. Minneapolis: Free Spirit Publishing, 2014. Print.

Stebbins, Leslie. *Finding Reliable Information Online: Adventures of an Information Sleuth*. Lanham, MD: Rowman & Littlefield, 2015. Print.

Willard, Nancy E. *Cyber Savvy: Embracing Digital Safety and Civility*. Thousand Oaks, CA: Corwin, 2012. Print.

WEBSITES

To learn more about Essential Library of the Information Age, visit **booklinks.abdopublishing.com**. These links are routinely monitored and updated to provide the most current information available.

FOR MORE INFORMATION

For more information on this subject, contact or visit the following organizations:

American Library Association

50 East Huron Street
Chicago, IL 60611
1-800-545-2433
http://www.ala.org/

The American Library Association was established to provide leadership for librarians. As such, this group is at the cutting edge of information literacy in the digital age.

Library of Congress

101 Independence Ave SE
Washington, DC 20540
1-202-707-5000
https://www.loc.gov/

The Library of Congress is the largest library in the world. It contains millions of books, images, and recordings.

Project Information Literacy

University of Washington
The Information School
PO Box 352840
Mary Gates Hall, Suite 370
Seattle, WA 98195-2840
1-206-685-9937
http://projectinfolit.org/

Project Information Literacy conducts ongoing research to determine how young adults seek information in the digital age and how they determine credibility, authority, relevance, and timeliness.

SOURCE NOTES

CHAPTER 1. LITERACY IN THE INFORMATION AGE

1. Eastern Gateway CCTS. "Information Literacy: Why It Is Important." Online video clip. *YouTube*. YouTube, 14 Jan. 2015. Web. 17 Sept. 2015.

2. *Gullible.info*. Gullible.info, 19 Sept. 2004. Web. 23 Dec. 2015.

3. *National Forum on Information Literacy*. National Forum on Information Literacy, Inc., n.d. Web. 21 Sept. 2015.

4. "Presidential Proclamation National Information Literacy Awareness Month." *The White House*. The United States Government, 1 Oct. 2009. Web. 21 Sept. 2015.

CHAPTER 2. THE HISTORY OF LITERACY

1. Jack Lynch. "Every Man Able to Read." *Colonial Williamsburg*. The Colonial Williamsburg Foundation, n.d. Web. 1 Oct. 2015.

2. Edward E. Gordon and Elaine H. Gordon. "Literacy – A Historical Perspective." *NAASP*. National Association of Secondary School Principals, Nov. 2003. Web. 1 Oct. 2015.

3. Ibid

4. "120 Years of Literacy." *National Center for Education Statistics*. US Department of Education, n.d. Web. 15 Oct. 2015.

5. "National Assessment of Adult Literacy—Key Findings." *National Assessment of Adult Literacy*. National Center for Education Statistics, n.d. Web. 29 Feb. 2016.

6. Lauren Browning. "We sent men to the moon in 1969 on a tiny fraction of the data that's in the average laptop." *Business Insider – Tech*. Business Insider Inc., 9 June 2015. Web. 1 Oct. 2015.

7. Ibid.

8. Kathryn Zickuhr. "Reading, writing, and research in the digital age." *Pew Research Center*. Pew Research Center, 4 Nov. 2013. Web. 15 Oct. 2015.

9. Andrew Perrin and Maeve Duggan. "Americans' Internet Access: 2000-2015." *Pew Research Center*. Pew Research Center, 26 June 2015. Web. 15 Oct. 2015.

10. Ibid.

11. Ibid.

12. Ibid.

13. "Presidential Committee on Information Literacy: Final Report." *ACRL*. ALA American Library Association, 10 Jan. 1989. Web. 21 Sept. 2015.

14. "H.R. 751 (102nd): National Literacy Act of 1991." *Govtrack.us*. Civic Impulse, LLC., 25 July 1991. Web. 15 Oct. 2015.

15. Monica Anderson. "Technology Device Ownership: 2015." *Pew Research Center.* Pew Research Center, 29 Oct. 2015. Web. 17 Nov. 2015.

16. Ibid.

17. Kristen Purcell et al. "How Teens do Research in the Digital World – Part III: The Changing Definition of 'Research.'" *Pew Research Center.* Pew Research Center, 1 Nov. 2012. Web. 1 Oct. 2015.

18. Ibid.

19. Ibid

CHAPTER 3. THE NEW FACE OF INFORMATION

1. David Russell Schilling. "Knowledge Doubling Every 12 Months, Soon to be Every 12 Hours." *Industry Tap.* Industry Tap, 19 Apr. 2013. Web. 5 Oct. 2015.

2. Ibid.

3. Ibid.

4. "Mobile Apps Usage – Statistics and Trends." *GO-Globe.* GO-Globe, 26 May 2015. Web. 17 Oct. 2015.

5. Ibid.

6. John B. Horrigan. "Chapter 1: Who Uses Libraries and What They do at Their Libraries." *Pew Research Center.* Pew Research Center, 15 Sept. 2015. Web. 1 Oct. 2015.

7. Ibid.

8. Kathryn Zickuhr, Lee Rainie, and Kristen Purcell. "Younger Americans' Library Habits and Expectations." *Pew Research Center.* Pew Research Center, 25 June 2013. Web. 17 Oct. 2015.

9. Holly Korbey. "In the Digital Age, What Becomes of the Library?" *Mind/Shift.* KQED News, 31 May 2013. Web. 23 Dec. 2015.

CHAPTER 4. FINDING THE CORRECT INFORMATION

1. Kathryn Zickuhr. "Reading, writing, and research in the digital age." *Pew Research Center.* Pew Research Center, 4 Nov. 2013. Web. 1 Oct. 2015.

2. Ibid.

3. Kristen Purcell, et al. "Part II: The Mixed Impact of Digital Technologies on Student Research." *Pew Research Center.* Pew Research Center, 1 Nov. 2012. Web. 18 Oct. 2015.

4. "Alan Emtage: The Man Who Invented The World's First Search Engine (But Didn't Patent It)." *Huff Post Tech.* TheHuffingtonPost.com, Inc., 1 Apr. 2013. Web. 15 Oct. 2015.

5. TED Talks. "Eli Pariser: Beware Online 'Filter Bubbles.'" Video. *YouTube.* YouTube, Feb. 2011. Web. 5 Oct. 2015.

SOURCE NOTES CONT.

6. Charles Seife. *Virtual Unreality.* New York: Viking/The Penguin Group, 2014. Print. 28–29.

7. TED Talks. "Eli Pariser: Beware Online 'Filter Bubbles.'" Video. *YouTube.* YouTube, Feb. 2011. Web. 5 Oct. 2015.

8. Kristen Purcell and Lee Rainie. "Americans Feel Better Informed Thanks to the Internet." *Pew Research Center.* Pew Research Center, 8 Dec. 2014. Web. 18 Oct. 2015.

9. Ibid.

10. Ibid.

11. Ibid.

CHAPTER 5. CRITICAL EVALUATION

1. Carl Heine and Dennis O'Connor. *Teaching Information Fluency.* Lanham, MD: The Scarecrow Press, Inc., 2014. Print. 41, 84–85.

2. Melissa Bell and Elizabeth Flock. "'A Gay Girl in Damascus' comes clean." *The Washington Post.* The Washington Post, 12 June 2011. Web. 16 Nov. 2015.

3. *Help Save the ENDANGERED Pacific Northwest Tree Octopus from EXTINCTION!* ZPi, n.d. Web. 15 Nov. 2015.

4. "Donald J. Leu – New Literacies Research Lab." *YouTube.* YouTube, 2 Mar. 2014. Web. 16 Nov. 2015.

CHAPTER 6. LEARNING HOW TO SHARE IN THE DIGITAL AGE

1. Janna Anderson and Lee Rainie. "Digital Life in 2025." *Pew Research Center.* Pew Research Center, 11 Mar. 2014. Web. 18 Oct. 2015.

2. Erin Skarda. "What You Need to Know About the 5 Most Successful Social Media Campaigns for Social Change." *NationSwell.* NationSwell, 16 Sept. 2014. Web. 16 Nov. 2015.

3. Vivek Ranadivé. "Hyperconnectivity: The Future is Now." *Forbes – Entrepreneurs.* Forbes.com, 19 Feb. 2013. Web. 19 Oct. 2015.

4. Joe Yogerst. "The Power of Social Networks." *Los Angeles Times.* Los Angeles Times, 15 Nov. 2013. Web. 19 Oct. 2015.

5. "The ALS Ice Bucket Challenge: The Impact of Social Media on Health Communication." *Tufts University School of Medicine.* Tufts Public Health, 18 Sept. 2014. Web. 16 Nov. 2015.

CHAPTER 7. ETHICS AND RESPONSIBILITY

1. Joe Karaganis and Lennart Renkema. "Copy Culture in the US & Germany." *The American Assembly.* Columbia University, 2013. Web. 17 Nov. 2015.

2. Alex Suskind. "15 Years After Napster: How the Music Service Changed the Industry." *The Daily Beast.* The Daily Beast Company, 6 June 2014. Web. 18 Oct. 2015.

3. U.S. Const. art. I, § 8, cl. 8.

4. "Musicians Sound Off on Napster." *USA Today – Tech Reviews.* USA Today, 6 Feb. 2002. Web. 20 Oct. 2015.

5. Sameer Hinduja, PhD and Justin W. Patchin, PhD. "State Cyberbullying Laws." *Cyberbullying Research Center.* Cyberbullying Research Center, July 2015. Web. 18 Oct. 2015.

6. "Cyberbullying Quotes." *NoBullying. com.* NoBullying.com, 6 Jan. 2015. Web. 20 Oct. 2015.

CHAPTER 8. SIGNIFICANT EFFECTS OF TECHNOLOGY

1. "How Brandi McWilliams Teaches with iPad." *Apple.* Apple, Inc., n.d. Web. 20 Oct. 2015.

2. Janna Anderson and Lee Rainie. "Digital Life in 2025." *Pew Research Center.* Pew Research Center, 11 Mar. 2014. Web. 21 Oct. 2015.

CHAPTER 9. THE FUTURE OF LITERACY

1. Thomas P. Mackey and Trudi E. Jacobson. *Metaliteracy: Reinventing Information Literacy to Empower Learners.* Chicago: American Library Association, 2014. Print. 106–107.

2. Kristen Purcell, et al. "Part IV: Teaching Research Skills in Today's Digital Environment." *Pew Research Center.* Pew Research Center, 1 Nov. 2012. Web. 18 Oct. 2015.

3. "Staggering Illiteracy Statistics." *Literacy Project Foundation.* The Literacy Project, n.d. Web. 15 Oct. 2015.

4. Ibid.

5. "How Dr. Craig Roble Teaches with iPad." *Apple.* Apple, Inc., n.d. Web. 20 Nov. 2015.

6. Terence P. Jeffrey. "In 23 Advanced Economies: US Adults Rank 21st in Math Skills." *Cnsnew.com.* Media Research Center, 18 Oct. 2013. Web. 15 Oct. 2015.

7. Council of Economic Advisors. "Mapping the Digital Divide." *The White House.* US Government, July 2015. Web. 17 Nov. 2015.

8. Ibid.

9. Alison J. Head and John Wihbey. "At Sea in a Deluge of Data." The Chronicle of Higher Education, 7 July 2014. Web. 15 Oct. 2015.

10. Ibid.

11. "Introduction to Information Literacy." *American Library Association.* American Library Association, n.d. Web. 21 Sept. 2015.

12. Council of Economic Advisors. "Mapping the Digital Divide." *The White House.* US Government, July 2015. Web. 17 Nov. 2015.

INDEX

ABOUT THE AUTHOR

Laura Perdew is an author, writing consultant, and former middle school teacher. She writes fiction and nonfiction for children, including numerous titles for the education market. She is also the author of *Kids on the Move! Colorado*, a guide to traveling through Colorado with children. Laura lives and plays in Boulder, Colorado, with her husband and twin boys.